paint pictures of Medusa.   No one knows what she really looked like, so we paint them any way we want.   Hoot! Hoot!

For Peter Henry Bates Martin

Dear Parents, Teachers, and Librarians,

This story was first told by the Greeks thousands of years ago. It was later written down by a Roman writer named Ovid (AH-vid). Since then, many writers have retold the myth. I have adapted it for children.

After reading this story a few times, children can take parts and read it like a play. Greek plays often had people on the side, commenting on the action. These people were called the "Greek chorus." I have chosen owls to be the Greek chorus in this book. Please read their words last, just before you turn the page.

Jean Marzollo

Special thanks to Bill Mayer, professor of Classical Studies at Hunter College, New York City; Dr. Joanne Marien, superintendent of Somers School District in Somers, New York; Shelley Thornton; Susan Jeffers; my agent Molly Friedrich; Cat Guthrie; Keaton and Joel Goss; Claudio Marzollo; Dan Marzollo; Dave Marzollo; Jesse Merandy; Patricia Adams; Irene O'Garden; Mim Galligan; Sheila Rauch; Julianne Gherardi; the helpful folks at Little, Brown; and all the children, teachers, and librarians at Otisville Elementary School in Otisville, New York, Primrose School in Somers, New York, and Haldane School in Cold Spring, New York.

Little, Brown and Company • Time Warner Book Group
1271 Avenue of the Americas, New York, NY 10020
Visit our Web site at www.lb-kids.com

First Edition: July 2006

ISBN 0-316-74136-1

10 9 8 7 6 5 4 3 2 1

SC

Printed in China

The illustrations for this book were painted in watercolor
and Chinese ink, then scanned and assembled like a collage in
Adobe Photoshop on a Power Mac G4. The text was set
in Hadriano Bold and Kid Print, and the
display type was set in Galahad.

The ancient Greeks drew pictures on vases. Why did they do that? They didn't have paper. Are we in this story?

GREEK MYTH
rated by JEAN MARZOLLO

Let's Go, Pegasus!

LITTLE, BROWN AND COMPANY
New York ∿ Boston

Yes, we're the Greek chorus!   What's that?   We listen to what's going on and then we talk about it.   Hoot! Hoot!

Once upon a time, a boy named Perseus lived on a Greek island with his mother, Danae. They were happy until one day when the mean and wicked king of the island came to visit. The king had an announcement.

Danae, I have chosen lucky
YOU to be my new wife!
Now, where's your son?
I have a job for him.

Danae doesn't seem too happy about marrying the king.   Her son, Perseus, doesn't like the idea either.   Hoot! Hoot!

The king didn't care if Danae didn't want to marry him. He was king. He could do whatever he wanted. The king knew that Danae's son, Perseus, didn't like him, so the king decided to get rid of him in a very sneaky way.

Perseus, I hear you are very brave. I command you to kill the monster Medusa and bring me her head. You wouldn't be afraid to do that, now, would you, my boy?

I'm not afraid of anything! If I kill this monster, will you agree to NOT marry my mother?

The king laughed a sneaky laugh and agreed.

Don't you think Perseus should have found out what kind of monster Medusa is before he said he would kill it? *Hoot! Hoot!*

Is that what the King wants?
To have Medusa turn me into a stone statue?
I'd better ask the gods for help.

How many Greek gods are there?   Twelve.   Hoot! Hoot!

The Greek gods lived way up high in the clouds on
Mount Olympus. Each god had special powers.
As the goddess of wisdom, Athena helped
people be brave and wise. She had a pet
owl. The god Hermes helped travelers.
He had wings on his hat and boots.

Dear gods on Mount Olympus,
Please help me be brave
on this journey! Please
don't let Medusa turn
me into a statue!

There are twelve gods, but only two are listening to Perseus.   Two is enough when it comes to Greek gods!   Hoot! Hoot!

Athena and Hermes flew down to Earth. Hermes gave Perseus a sword to cut off Medusa's head and also a red stretchy bag for carrying the head. Athena let Perseus use her shield.

Medusa has snakes for hair! But don't worry about that, Perseus. Worry about her eyes. The second Medusa looks into your eyes, you will turn to stone. To protect yourself, use my shield as a mirror. Look only at Medusa's reflection in the mirror.

Okay.

Hermes handed Perseus a pair of winged boots. He explained that Medusa's island was too far away to go there by boat.

You can fly there instead! Just put on these boots and hop up into the air— like this!

Perseus put the sword in his belt and his left arm in the straps of the shield. Then he counted, "One, two, three, hop!" He was a little wobbly at first, but soon Perseus could walk and leap through the sky.

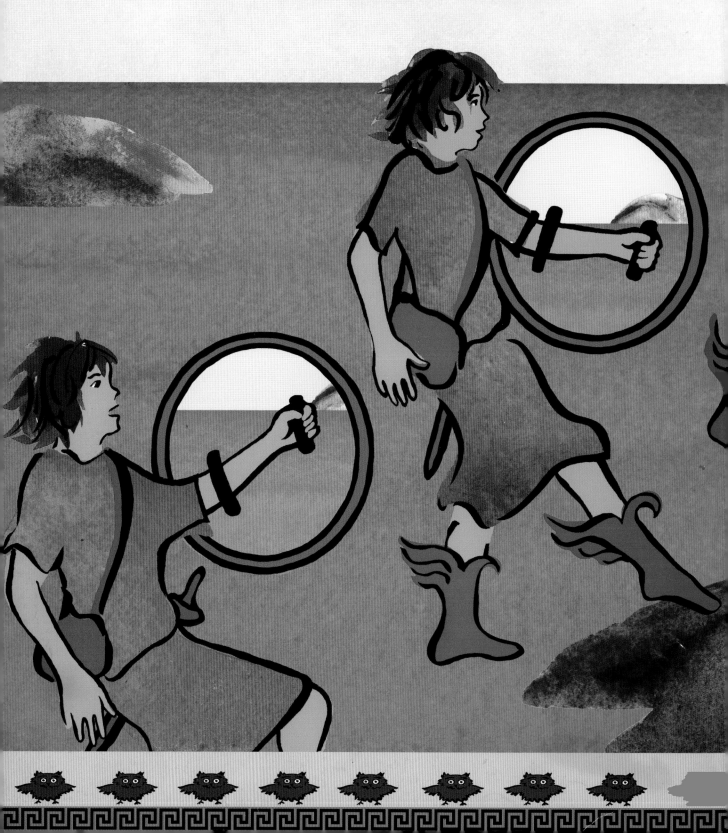

I can leap over land and sea!
Medusa, Medusa, you don't scare me!

Perseus is flying—just like Pegasus! Hey, where is Pegasus? He comes later. You have to be patient. *Hoot! Hoot!*

Perseus landed on Medusa's island and used his shield as a mirror, just as Athena had told him to do. He saw Medusa running and hiding behind stone statues of people and animals. She spoke to him playfully.

Medusa's voice was friendly.
Maybe she wasn't evil.
She seemed to want to play.
Should Perseus turn around
and talk to her?

Perseus decided to turn his body but NOT his head. That was wise, because now Medusa was running straight at him. With his heart beating fiercely, Perseus kept his eyes on the shield and held out his sword. When Medusa came close enough, he swung his sword around and cut off her head.

Medusa's head went flying and
landed in the grass by the cow.

Moo!

Hey, look! The cow came to life!   Will the other statues come to life, too?   Turn the page!   Hoot! Hoot!

Hermes had told Perseus to put Medusa's head in the bag carefully because her eyes would still be able to turn people to stone. As he was doing that, Perseus heard happy noises. Looking up, he saw that all the statues were people and animals again.

Out of Medusa's body rose a beautiful white horse with wings.
The horse gave Perseus a look, as if to say, "Well, what are you waiting
for?" Perseus leaped upon it, and together they flew into the sky.

Bow wow!

Let's go, Pegasus! Now you're free!
From death came life, as all can see!

Neigh!

Ribbit!

When the wicked king spotted Perseus arriving home on Pegasus, he tried to run away, but he didn't get far. Perseus lifted Medusa's head from the bag, just high enough so that Medusa's eyes looked right at the king. *ZAP!* The wicked king became a statue and never bothered anyone ever again.

Danae was truly overjoyed to see her son.

Dear, dear Perseus. I'm so glad you're safe—and I'm so proud of you! You saved me from the king! Tell us everything! Where did you get that horse?

Athena and Hermes look pleased.   That's because Perseus is a hero, and they helped him.   He helped himself, too.   *Hoot! Hoot!*

People wanted Perseus to be king, but Perseus said no. He knew his power belonged to the gods. Now it was time to return it.

Athena put Medusa's head on her shield. Thanks to Perseus, Medusa's power to destroy was now Athena's power to help people be brave and wise.

Do Medusa's eyes still work? Only when Athena wants them to. As the goddess of wisdom, she makes good decisions. Hoot! Hoot!

Which Medusa painting was used in this book?   I'm going to paint another Medusa!   I'm going to paint Pegasus!